Environmental Change
and Integration of Power into
Organizational Learning Processes

Environmental Change and Integration of Power into Organizational Learning Processes

Sadra Mirmohammadi

To order additional copies of this book, contact:
Xlibris Corporation
1-888-795-4274
www.Xlibris.com
Orders@Xlibris.com
89892

Contents

Abstract

A model in which organizational learning results from interaction at three levels (individual, group, and organization) through 4I processes is developed by incorporating a political dimension. According to this political dimension, organizational learning 4I processes (intuition, interpretation, integration, and institutionalization) are connected to systemic and episodic forms of power. These processes are linked to discipline, influence, force, and domination, in that order. We examined the learning practices of companies in a non-Western economy under strong environmental pressure to learn from previous experiences with the least amount of trial and error. We analyze the linked assumptions and logic underlying learning processes for a project, and the integration of power into the 4I framework. We confirm the proposition of a 4I framework, although some aspects may require modification. In particular we find that systemic pressures may not necessarily lie within the confines of the focal organization.

Keywords: institutionalization, intuition, interpretation, integration, systemic power, episodic power.

1. Introduction

This paper examines organizational learning (OL) in the context of an organization in a developing non-Western economy. We apply key insights from the literature to shed light on how significant OL took place in an Iranian power industry organization as a result of implementing the first non-turnkey power plant in the country. In our analysis we combine case studies with statistical surveys. Our main objective was to examine the OL process that resulted from project implementation to investigate whether it conforms to the influential process models suggested by Crossan et al. and Lawrence et al. (2005) that use a framework within which OL results. Interactions occur at three levels: individual, group and organizational. In this framework the OL process begins with individual learning, namely through individual 'intuition', which is then transformed to the group and organizational levels through interpretative and integrative processes, respectively. Whilst the so-called 4I framework represents a descriptive/analytical OL process, the contribution of Lawrence et al. is to develop a framework that incorporates a political dimension, which helps to indicate which particular ideas or innovations may shape OL in an organization. In distinguishing between systemic and episodic power, Lawrence et al. (2005) argue that different forms of organizational power are likely to be operative in each of the processes that link learning between individual, group, and organizational levels.

The remainder of the paper is organized as follows.

In section 2 we give a brief overview of the literature on OL.

Section 3 discusses the contribution of process views, concentrating on the contributions of Crossan et al. [1999] and Lawrence et al. (2005).

Section 4 briefly sets out the context and background to the empirical study.

In Section 5 we explain the methodological approach adopted in the study. Section 6 reports findings from interviews of managers and questionnaire surveys of several hundred operatives who experienced implementation of power plant projects by Tavanir.

In Section 7 we discuss the results of the interviews and questionnaire surveys in light of the theoretical contributions examined in Section 3. We argue that while the Tavanir experience largely confirms the propositions of the 4I framework, there are aspects that may require modification.

2. Conceptual background

As a starting point, we adopt the definition of OL offered by Dixon (1994, p. 77) as: "The intentional use of learning processes at the individual, group and system level to continuously transform the organization in a direction that is increasingly satisfying to its stakeholders". "Intention" has a positive effect on learning outcomes.

Whilst this is probably true at both the individual and organizational levels, intention is a more salient and distinctive part of the process for organizations. In a sense, intention takes cognizance of the multi-layer nature of organizations. If we assume that learning within an organization is mostly initiated at the individual level, as in the case in the 4I framework developed by Crossan et al (1999, p. 356), for example, then its development into group and organizational learning is more effective if these processes are intentionally shaped and/or managed. We acknowledge that all organizations learn to a greater or lesser extent. They adapt to environmental constraints, prevent the repetition of past mistakes, and generate innovative and new ideas. However, although such OL occurs, equally typically, there are situations in which learning is not achieved; intentional processes facilitate OL at individual, group and system levels. The OL process involves the construction and reconstruction of meaning, and as such is a dynamic process (Crossan et al. 1999, p. 532) that feeds forward and back through individual, group and organization levels. Each process is viewed as a cycle of four steps:

(a) the widespread generation of information;
(b) the integration of new information into the organizational context;
(c) collective interpretation of the information; and

(d) authorization of organizational members to take responsible action based on the interpreted meaning. The fourth step then feeds back into the first to generate new information.

Bell et al. (2002) identified four principal schools of OL research: an economic view, a developmental view, a managerial view, and a process view. Each school agrees that the total sum of an individual's knowledge, understanding, and memory contributes significantly to the overall learning of the organization, although "the individuals have some components which are not known or accessible to the organization" (Argyris and Schon, 1978; Hedberg, 1981, p. 6; Fiol and Lyles, 1985; Easterby-Smith, 2000, p. 785).

The process school, however, goes further than this, arguing that individual learning processes are replicated at a macro level to produce organizational cognition (Bell et al., 2002, p. 78). Learning processes effective at the individual level may be at work within the organization, leading to organization-wide learning (Kim, 1993, p. 42). Also, an underlying tenet of the process school is that learning is grounded in the cognitive and behavioral capabilities of individual members. The process view also argues that learning is a socially constructed phenomenon.

3. The 4I framework

Crossan et al. (1999) proposed a framework for understanding the nature of OL that stresses a three-stage dynamic process. This approach, known as the 4I framework, highlights asserted 'intuiting' and 'interpreting' processes at the individual level, 'integrating' processes under the group level, and finally 'institutionalizing' to inform the organizational level. Following Bontis et al. (2002, p. 439), we can usefully distinguish 'stocks' of knowledge residing at the three levels (individual, group and organizational) from the flow of learning across levels to create feed-forward and feedback between the levels.

The 4I framework (Crossan et al., 1999) has three characteristics important in the development of a general model of OL: (1) it is multilevel; (2) it is dynamic; and (3) it clearly involves four processes—intuiting, interpreting, integrating, and institutionalizing (the 4Is)—that allow learning to feed forward from the individual through the group level to the organizational level and feed back to the individual level.

Moreover, these levels are connected by bi-directional processes that involve both the creation and application of knowledge (Lawrence et al., 2005, p. 181).

Intuiting is carried out by individuals, who develop novel insights (Bontis et al., 2002; Crossan et al., 1999) based on their experience and their ability to ascertain underlying or potential patterns, and then translate those insights into metaphors for communication (Lawrence et al., 2005, p. 181).

Interpreting is the next step in OL, defined as "the explaining, through words and/or actions, of an insight or idea to one's self and to others" (Crossan et al., 1999, p. 525).

Daft and Weick (1984, p. 286) formally defined interpretation as the process of translating events and developing shared understanding and conceptual schemes among members of upper management. Through interpreting, individuals develop cognitive maps of various domains in which they operate. Interpreting requires more than competence and capabilities, and, according to Bontis et al. (2002), requires both motivation and direction or focus. Watkin and Marsik (1993) stated that interpreting is the nexus between an individual's capability, motivation and focus that enhances that individual's learning. Focus is what individuals need to do and may be enhanced by what they want to do, their motivation, or other unknown factors.

Integrating is the third process of Crossan et al. (1999) and is the first that occurs at the group level. It is "the process of developing shared understanding among individuals and of taking coordinated action through mutual adjustment" (Crossan et al., 1999, p. 525).

Institutionalizing is the fourth process, which, according to Lawrence et al. (2005), is the learning that has occurred among individuals and groups and is embedded into the organization through "systems, structures, procedures, and strategies" (Crossan et al., 1999, p. 525). Together, these four processes form a learning loop through the effect of new institutions on organizational members' experiences that feed into their individual intuitions (Lawrence et al., 2005, p. 181).

3.1 Integrating power into the 4I framework

According to Lawrence et al. (2005), any theory of OL without an understanding of its political dynamics will always be incomplete, because organizations are inherently political and, consequently, so are the processes of OL. They also asserted that bringing power and politics into research on OL should provide a more effective foundation for understanding why some organizations are better able to learn. They also suggested that only some of the available innovations are embraced by organizations and bringing politics into research helps to understand why. More specifically, Lawrence et al. (2005) extended the multilevel procession framework model of OL developed by Crossan et al. (1999). They stated that although this framework provides a compelling basis for research on OL, it neglects the role of power and politics and, consequently, is insufficient for addressing which new ideas will be transformed into organizational institutions and which institutions will provide the basis for further intuitions.

The issue of understanding which ideas will be integrated into group activities and which will be institutionalized in organizations, as well as the transformation of new ideas to coherent and collective action, depends on the actions of interested actors who work to embed them in the routines, structures, and culture of organizations. The success of these 'institutional entrepreneurs' is significantly affected by their access to the right resources and their skills in leveraging such resources.

3.2 Power politics and Organizational learning (OL)

Taken together, the four processes of OL highlight the importance of understanding the role of power and politics in OL. Lawrence et al (2005) suggested that intuiting, interpreting, integrating, and institutionalizing constitute the basic elements of OL, but that without a theory of the political dynamics that support those processes, a general theory of OL will always be incomplete and unable to fully explain or predict which new ideas evolve from intuition to institutions.

Lawrence et al. (2005, p. 182) emphasized two distinct modes of power, episodic and systemic. They argued that although power is still defined narrowly in managerial theory and research, these two modes of power have distinct implications for OL. Episodic power refers to discrete and strategic political acts initiated by self-interested actors. In contrast, systemic forms of power act through the routine ongoing practices of an organization (Lawrence et al., 2005). Rather than being held by autonomous actors, systemic forms of power are diffused throughout the social systems that constitute organizations.

Connecting episodic and systemic power to the OL processes of Crossan et al. (1999) provides a foundation for understanding how politics affects OL. These connections only begin, however, to address the issue of predicting which ideas will proceed successfully through each of the OL processes (Lawrence et al., 2005). Greater understanding requires examination of the specific political processes that are tied most tightly to each learning process and the resources on which they depend. Lawrence et al. (2005) drew on this typology to examine the political processes associated with each stage of the OL cycle.

Their ideas are briefly overviewed in the remainder of this section.

3.3 The politics of interpretation

Referring to the idea of Crossan et al. (1999) that "the communication of ideas to others occurs through a process of interpreting that allows individuals' ideas to be shared with others", Lawrence et al. (2005) suggested that this feature highlights the precariousness of the process. We have already discussed the interpretation process of OL. This process occurs in relation to an environment that rewards particular interpretations and penalizes others (Daft and Weick, 1984), but does so in a highly ambiguous manner. As a result, interested actors will exploit this ambiguity by using political strategies to affect the language and cognitive maps that others adopt and construct (Lawrence et al., 2005).

According to Crossan et al. (1999), the interpretation of a new idea is a social process in which members construct new cognitive maps. Although any form of power might be evident in any of the four processes, we believe that the form of power most effective during interpretation is influence, which affects the costs and benefits that organizational members associate with specific interpretations of a new idea (Lawrence et al., 2005).

Influence is associated with the interpretation of new ideas for two reasons. First, influence affects the costs and benefits of action; and second, the precise language and cognitive maps that will ultimately describe a new idea are likely to emerge in somewhat organic and unpredictable ways over time which would make force (the other form of episodic power) problematic (Lawrence et al., 2005).

According to Lawrence et al. (2005), three factors are critical for effective influence, depending on the tactics of actors: (1) control of scarce resources; (2) domain-relevant expertise; and (3) culturally appropriate social skills. Considering that organizations are political arenas in which multiple actors may be engaged and where the use of influence will often be met by political opposition, Lawrence et al. (2005) developed their first proposition: "The interpretation of a new idea will be best facilitated by a political strategy that involves the use of influence and is based on access to scarce resources, relevant expertise, and/or culturally appropriate social skills".

3.4 The politics of integration

Ideas must be championed at opportune moments and affirmed during moments of doubt to be integrated effectively at the group level. Lawrence et al. (2005) emphasized the ability of some organizational members to restrict the range of actions available to others, accepting the ability of individual actions to direct through "influence". They argued that force will be the most effective political means to integrate new ideas into group activities and that innovations, to move to the organization level, must be brought to the attention of senior management at appropriate times and, in many cases, revisited on numerous occasions. The use of force in organizations is tied much more closely to formal organizational hierarchies, as suggested by their second proposition: The integration of a new idea into group activities will best be facilitated by a political strategy that involves the use of force based on formal authority.

3.5 The politics of institutionalization

Crossan et al. (1999) argued that the institutionalization of ideas leverages the learning of individuals and groups by embedding new ideas into the procedures and systems that structure organizational life. Although the concept of systemic power begins to address this issue, which new ideas will become institutionalized involves the movement of ideas from the organization to the individuals (Lawrence et al., 2005). Institutionalization depends on a mode of power that can maintain new ideas as part of organizational life without repeated intervention by interested actors. In contrast to interpretation and integration, institutionalization can be problematic because it may be implicated in groups in which the innovation has no champion or detractors. For this reason, Lawrence et al. (2005) suggested that "fully institutionalizing innovations within an organization requires their incorporation within systemic forms of power". To overcome potential resistance to institutionalization, a better way is to restrict the range of available action.

Lawrence et al. (2005) believed that domination affects organizational members' behavior, limiting their preferences, attitudes, and beliefs. This may have negative connotations, leading to a potentially coercive environment can be enabling, productive, and enjoyable for the members affected.

The Third proposition of Lawrence et al. (2005) is: "The institutionalization of an innovation will best be facilitated by a political strategy that involves systems of domination".

3.6 The politics of intuition

Crossan et al. (1999, p. 528) argued that intuition is an OL process whereby individuals come to discern and comprehend something new; individuals recognize patterns in their experience, which allows them to imagine new solutions or opportunities. A major factor in the experience of organizational members is the set of structures, procedures, and systems that organize their working lives and provide context for this experience (Lawrence et al., 2005). In recent work on systemic forms of power, researchers have highlighted the ways in which power can affect not only the behavior of individuals, but also their perception and imagination (Lawrence et al., 2005). Thus, Lawrence et al. argued that "both institutionalizing new ideas and establishing those ideas as the basis for further intuitions will depend primarily on systemic forms of power".

Lawrence et al. (2005) argued that the political dynamic of intuition involves forms of power that help organizational member to gain expertise, and discipline is the most effective form of power in this regard, and thus is the key political basis of intuition.

Discipline, they believed, involves an ongoing systemic engagement with the target of power and affects the actions of organizational members by shaping their understanding of the costs and benefits of different behavior and courses of action. Lawrence et al. (2005) suggested that "disciplinary systems support the development of expertise through the establishment of routine organizational systems that can provide individual members with deep levels of substantive experience in a domain . . . fostering intuition". Unlike influence, Lawrence et al. argued, discipline focuses on shaping the actual formation of members' identity and provides them with psychological and discursive resources that help them to relate to the organizational experience. The last proposition suggested by Lawrence et al. (2005) is: "The fostering of intuitions that are consistent with and extend an innovation will be facilitated by a political strategy that involves systems of discipline providing deep levels of experience and consistent bases for identity formation".

4. Case study of the role of power and politics in OL

4.1 Historical background

As a governmental organization, Tavanir conducts construction projects. In the aftermath of events in 1979, the combined impacts of the Iranian Islamic revolution, war and economic sanctions affected the environmental sustainability of business under the influence of multiple pressures such as changes in regulations, social desirability, and national bias. This prompted Iranian companies (including Tavanir) to adopt policies and organizational systems to support employees with the most innovative and creative actions. The critical consequences for Tavanir were as follows.

4.1.1 New politics-led employee innovations

The motivational stance of Tavanir managers and workers was significantly affected by the changing conditions. These conditions instilled a belief in Tavanir personnel that their work was a vital part of national defense and survival. This belief was buttressed by the strong religious conviction of the new management strata in Tavanir, for whom survival of the Islamic republic was a vital additional consideration, by creative ideas proposed by individuals and/or teams, and by creative behaviors.

4.1.2 Management power resulting from new politics

Tavanir management anticipated that the 1980 sanctions would remain in force for a long time. Decreases in the price and production of oil automatically prompted management to change their approach in a way that enabled them to sustain their business in terms of more efficient resources and services. These conditions led managers to change past behavior, choosing new politics for administration.

Tavanir established a new department to take overall charge of the SRPP[power plant under research] project (the SRPP department) and consider the findings and recommendations of the Tavanir center of excellence. The SRPP department had enhanced managerial authority and extensive organizational and financial facilities. Managerial behaviors that led to feelings of self-efficacy contributed to higher subordinate creativity (Ramus and Steger, 2000), which was also influenced by the new politics resulting from new managerial behavior and an open approach to decision-making.

This policy clearly demonstrates the role of management supervisory support in employee empowerment (Ramus and Steger, 2000, p. 9) and its motivational concept of self-efficacy, or employees' feelings that they can influence their own work.

4.1.3 Power-directed focus on OL

The technical committee provided a master plan to help all contractors and managers to improve their way of working and to increase their knowledge for implementation of other Iranian projects. Furthermore, the committee recommended a new organizational structure, methods and procedures to make learning possible. The committee also suggested that "a number of supervisors must be appointed in each project that is contractually committed to learning through participating in operational practices. These supervisors must report and reflect their learning to managers in every monthly meeting".

Tavanir used consulting engineering companies that were contractually committed to learn more when they supervising projects and to transfer new knowledge to the SRPP technical committee.

4.1.4 Effects of the model of power on OL

Under environmental pressures, Tavanir took the following steps. (1) Managers previewed new clauses in contracts to prepare contractors and new managers to accept such a big obligation by obtaining knowledge that they did not have at the time of contract signing. (2) All executive managers and contractors were committed to prepare learning conditions for their staff and to transfer learning matters to different work groups. (3) The center of excellence extended it's function to encouraging innovative and creative staff members in different work groups and subprojects to participate in efforts to solve their technical and managerial problems. (4) A supervisor company monitored the progress of different projects, innovative solutions and creative activities and reported to Tavanir on a monthly basis. (5) A monthly management meeting of all SRPP operational and supporting managers, members of the center of excellence and the supervisory company was set up. Problems and learning practices were discussed and then the committee approved procedures and working instructions to be adopted. SRPP senior management (strongly affected by the changed environment) created an impetus for organizational learning. We now describe the relationship of these steps to the politics of power.

4.2 Power of domination and institutionalization

SRPP senior management (step 2) prepared the first organizational plan. The details of each function were defined and groups of staff assigned to each function were agreed and contractually committed. The relationship between groups, managers and the center of excellence to obtain the best result for learning and transfer to others was contractually distinguished.

Those in charge of steps 1, 2, 3 and 5 (Section 4.1.4) used their resources and skills to leverage OL. In step 2, managers and contractors accepted the strong power of the new politics adopted by Tavanir senior management, concluded contracts, supported the plan involving structuring and grouping, and regularly reported to on another. In fact, in this stage Tavanir institutionalized past learning experiences by attracting and gathering the best experts from different projects using light shed by the center of excellence. We are clearly convinced that institutionalizing ideas and embedding them in the organization not only leveraged the learning of individuals and groups (Crossan et al., 1999), but also stabilized managers' intentions and goals to learn through formal contracts. We are also convinced that these contracts and environmental motivations prepared innovators, through systemic forms of power, to overcome potential resistance to institutionalization and restricted the range of available action (Lawrence et al., 2005) for everyone working in this project.

4.3 Power of discipline and intuition

SRPP workers and contractors were obliged to participate in different groups and transfer their innovative ideas to everyone interested in each subproject. The new politics adopted by management prepared everyone involved to think in terms of the new approach in fulfilling his/her duty. Innovative and creative ways were encouraged contractually and were fully structured and systemized in projects. The reward systems for learning and understanding the "costs and benefit of different behavior and courses of action" (Lawrence et al., 2005) provided SRPP members with deep levels of experience, allowing individuals to discern what they had not done before.

The SRPP provided organizational members with a structure and a set of systems and legal procedures that we believe prompted employees in this project to do their jobs based on institutionalized ideas, and also established those ideas as the basis for further intuitions.

As Lawrence et al. (2005) argued, this depends primarily on systemic forms of power.

We are convinced that in this project the systemic form of power that supported individuals with deep levels of substantive experience was discipline, which predominantly fostered and extended innovation in this project, thus facilitating the intuition process.

4.4 Power of interpretation and integration

Employees in the center of excellence were self-innovative people and used their creative ideas to help and encourage project employees and contractor staffs to innovate new ideas and creative actions. Step (2) above shows that employees were organized to work in groups with a very specific learning commitment. Whilst this group of people benefited from the advice of the center of excellence, the supervisory company (step 4) was responsible for supervising employee progress in learning.

As Lawrence et al. (2005) argued, "although any form of power might be evident in any of the four processes . . . the forms of power most effective during interpretation and integration are influence and force". In this project, the management intent to carry out the project through learning by doing meant that employees were highly supported and motivated to learn. However, we could not find enough evidence in this case that "influence" or "force" was more effective than other type of power during the processes of interpretation and integration.

4.5 Further evidence of support

We extended our work by submitting 20 questions from a previous questionnaire (Mirmohammadi, 2005, pp. 270-300) to 20 key managers in the SRPP. These questions, we believe, can distinguish the type of power effects on each of the processes of OL. We empirically tested which of the identified factors have a significant impact on OL (Tables 1 to 4 in the Appendix).

5. Methodology

Assuming that "how" and "why" questions are the focus of this study, a further distinction among history, case study, and experiment is the extent of the investigator's control over and access to actual behavioral events (Yin, 1994, p. 8). During this research, access to SRPP project data diaries, reports, evidence and documents provided evidence that the case study represented an exceptionally advantageous research opportunity. The results were strengthened by testing employee perceptions through "what" or "how much' questions developed at the end of case study.

The general aim of the study was to obtain variables that measured the view of employees in Tavanir power plants on crucial OL factors to check what type of power was more effective in each of the OL processes.

The methods used consisted of a large postal questionnaire and face-to-face questioning or interview. Both were used to yield descriptive statistics and sub-scale scores. The questionnaires were sent to a predetermined number of SRPP operating staff and to staff from four other power plants. We arranged a number of individual interviews with staff members who wished to complete the questionnaire but had problems in reading or understanding them.

The questionnaires were prepared in English and translated into Farsi by the author. The dual language questionnaires were checked by several competent English speakers to identify any weaknesses in translation. The text was then rechecked and errors were corrected. The statistical survey comprised a questionnaire instrument consisting of 20 statements (nos. 128-147) developed to assess learning organization specifics within Tavanir and the projects.

6. Statistical survey results

The questionnaire was administered to staff of power plant companies. There were a total of 450 questionnaires, of which 200 were administered to managers and experts and 250 to other staff chosen from more than 3000 employees. A total of 400 (88.88%) questionnaires were returned, of which 339 (74% of the total population) were usable. This sample is large enough to be free from sampling error (Cohen and Manion, 1994, pp. 80-95). Furthermore, all participants had sufficient information about the technical, financial and historical aspects of each of the components of the power plants.

Some limitations were encountered. Project staff in the power plants were not always accessible. This problem was overcome by choosing (1) different power operating companies and (2) almost all operating companies from the same construction project, including SRPP. This resulted in access to sufficient members of staff with experience in the projects under investigation.

The crucial OL factors reveal that respondents supported more or less all of the 20 statements, with high mean scores and uniformly low SDs. The highest mean is 3.5126 and the lowest is 1.7579. However, although all 20 statements were offered as OL preconditions and support all of the forms of politics affecting OL, the discussion considers more specific forms of power in OL processes.

7. Discussion

7.1 Systemic form of power

7.1.1 Statements most related to domination

In this part of survey, the existence of domination is supported by many statements, but more strongly by those in Table 1. Questions such as numbers 140 and 144 support the movement of ideas from the organization to the individuals, affecting their behavior, attitudes, and beliefs. Finally, staff preferences (for example, question 145) were limited to innovative work and helped to transfer what they learned to the organizational structures and procedures, ending in the process of institutionalization.

7.1.2 Statements most related to discipline

Five statements in Table 2, we believe, support the existence of the systemic power of discipline in this part of our study. We find that socialization and team-based work and intuition are supported by the staff view that the project was organized to gain the commitment of workers to develop new ideas and socialization (questions 128 and 129).

These items support other types of power to a certain degree, but are most related to discipline.

7.2. Episodic forms of power

7.2.1 Statements most related to influence

Statements in Table 3 support the role of influence. These views provide evidence that the project succeeded because openness and transparency were encouraged. In this case, transfer of knowledge was quick and efficient and people were motivated to share their ideas. Previous studies have highlighted the role of organizational encouragement of risk taking and idea generation and of valuing innovation at all levels of the organization (Cummings, 1965; Delbecq and Mills, 1985;

Kanter, 1983; Kimberley and Evanisko, 1981). These views, we believe, facilitated the interpretation of new ideas. These concepts could help in managing ambiguity and uncertainty in the adoption of language and construction of cognitive maps, and support the effects of influence in the process of interpretation.

7.2.2 Statements most related to force

Statements in Table 4 support the idea that some organizational members were able to limit the range of action available to facilitate the integration of new ideas into group activities. When employees concur with the view that their salary is better than for other projects, completion of the project will result in self-efficacy and self-sufficiency.

Moreover, employee experiences provided them with new skills, success was based on predicting the actions required, and completion of the project was necessary to satisfy national self-confidence. All of these factors support the need to force integration of new ideas across the workforce, resulting in collective action for implementation of the project.

8. Conclusions

This research involving a case study and statistical survey represents an initial step in identifying an empirically validated relationship between systemic and episodic forms of power and the willingness of managers and employees to promote OL in a developing country. A case study of a project, including interviews with more than 20 key managers and experts, revealed that key managers in Tavanir, who perceived strong environment signals, established a flexible technical and administrative system for transferring knowledge throughout the organization quickly and efficiently. This means that managers purposefully organized very motivated and skilled people to facilitate project implementation by learning. Managers introduced and promoted team learning and enhanced worker commitment to learn and to increase group knowledge.

This case study highlights the environmental changes experienced by Tavanir. Strong changes in staff and managerial views resulted from the new conditions. Moreover, the new situation allowed management to put more focus on developing learning processes without fear of reaction by staff. Environmental conditions also affected staff and prompted them to carry out their jobs better and to welcome any new strategy on learning or helping others to learn. Although individuals have some component that are not known or accessible to organizations (Argyris and Schon, 1978, p. 9; Hedberg, 1981, p. 6; Fiol and Lyles, 1985; Easterby-Smith, 2000, p. 785, results from our statistical survey indicate that employees responded positively to this idea. There was a strong linkage between the existence of a planned learning policy and the willingness of the staff to exhibit self-efficacy in learning and doing, demonstrating an increase in managers' power over different learning processes.

We clearly proved that institutionalizing ideas and embedding them in the organization not only leveraged the learning of individuals and groups, but also stabilized managers' intentions and goals to learn through formal contracts. Learning is a modification of behavior through activities and experiences, including modes of adjustment towards a changed environment (Carroll, 1996, p. 717), and we demonstrated that contracts and environmental motivations provided innovators with domination power to overcome potential resistance to institutionalization and to restrict the range of action available to everyone working in the project.

Regarding the effect of the power of discipline on the intuition process, we are convinced that disciplinary systems support the development of expertise through the establishment of routine organizational systems that can provide individual members with deep levels of substantive experience. In this study we found that managerial behaviors that led to feelings of self-efficacy contributed to higher subordinate creativity and that the creativity of subordinates was influenced by new politics resulting from new managerial behavior and an open approach to decision-making. The strategic policy in this project clearly demonstrates the role of supervisory management, which can influence an employee's work. In practice we found evidence that self-innovative employees were often operationalized using their creative ideas under the power of discipline or sets of structures, systems and legal procedures, and we believe that they used institutionalized ideas and established those ideas as the basis for further intuitions.

Even though the case study does not provide sufficient evidence that influence and force are more effective than other type of power during interpretation and integration, the support of statements in Tables 3 and 4 demonstrates the effects of influence on the interpretation process and of force on the integration process. We recommend further research to identify whether the acceptance by employees of both the systemic and episodic forms of power is relevant to managerial plans related to the organizational environment. We also recommend research to determine the impact of competence—building, communication, and management goals and responsibilities on the 4I process in terms of supervisory support and encouragement of the institutionalization of lessons learned from different organizations and departments. Although this study has demonstrated that the use of effective power cannot be fully complete without the intent of managers, future research is necessary on the synonymous managerial and 4I schools of thought in terms of the impact of the politics of power on OL.

References

Argyris, C., and Schon, D. A. (1978). Organizational Learning: A Theory of Action Perspective. Reading, MA: Addison-Wesley.

Argyris, C., and Schon, D. (1996). Organizational Learning II: Theory, Method, and Practice. Reading MA: Addison-Wesley.

Bapuji, H., and Crossan, M. (2004). From raising questions to providing answers: Reviewing organizational learning research. Management Learning 35(4): 397-417.

Bell, J. S., Withwell, J. Y., and Lukas, A. B. (2002). Schools of thought in organizational learning. Journal of the Academy of Marketing Science 30: 70-86.

Bontis, N., Crossan, M. M., and Hulland, J. (2002). Managing an organizational learning system by aligning stocks and flows. Journal of Management Studies 39(4): 437-469.

Carroll, J. S. (1998). Organizational learning activities in high-hazard industries: The logics underlying self-analysis. Journal of Management Studies 35(6): 699-717.

Cohen, W. M., and Manion, J. (1994). Research Methods in Education. London: Croom-Helm.

Crossan, M. M., Lane, H. W., and White, R. E. (1999). An organizational learning framework: From intuition to institution. Academy of Management Review 24(3): 522-537.

Crossan, M., Lane, H., White, R. E., and Djurfeldt, L. (1995). Organizational learning dimensions for a theory. International Journal of Organizational Analysis 3: 337-360.

Cummings, L. L. (1965). Organizational climates for creativity. Journal of the Academy of Management 3: 220-227.

Daft, R. L., and Weick, K. E. (1984). Toward a model of organizations as interpretation systems. Academy of Management Review 9(2): 284-295.

Dixon, N. M. (1994). The hallways of learning. Organizational Dynamics 25(4): 23-33.

Delbec, A. L., and Mills, P. K. (1985). Managerial practices that enhance innovation. Organizational Dynamics 14(1): 24-34.

Easterby-Smith, M. (2000). Organizational learning and mature culture: Do models of organizational learning apply outside USA? Separata del Boletin, Vol. l, 111/August, pp. 78-96

Fiol, C. M., and Lyles, M. A. (1985). Organisational learning. Academy of Management Review, 10(4): 803-813.

Hedberg, B. (1981). How organisations learn and unlearn. In: Handbook of Organisational Design, Vol. 1. Oxford: Oxford University Press, pp. 3-27.

Kanter, R. M. (1983). The Change Masters. New York: Simon & Schuster.

Kim, D. H. (1993). The link between individual and organizational learning. Sloan Management Review 35: 30-50.

Kimberly, R., and Evanisko, M. J. (1981). Organizational innovation: The influence of individual, organizational, and contextual factors on hospital adoption of technological and administrative innovations. Academy of Management Journal 24: 689-713.

Kolb, D. A., and Boyatzis, R. E. (1984). Goal-setting and self-directed behavior change. In: Organizational Psychology, 4th edition (edited by D. A. Kolb, I. M. Rubin and J. M. McIntyre). Engelwood Cliffs, NJ: Prentice Hall.

Lall, S. (1998). Technological capabilities in emerging Asia. Oxford Development Studies 26(2): 213-245.

Lawrence, B. T., Mauws, K. M., and Dyck, B. 2005. The politics of organizational learning: Integrating power into the 4I framework. Academy of Management Review 30: 180-191.

Mirmohammadi, S. (2005). Organizational learning in a power plant in Iran. PhD thesis, Manchester University, UK.

Ramus, C. A., and Steger, U. (2000). The role of supervisory support behaviors and environmental policy in employee "ecoinitiatives" at leading edge European companies. Academy of Management Journal 43(4): 605-626.

Ramus, C. A., and Steger, U. (2007). The role of supervisory support behaviors and environmental policy in employee eco-initiatives and leading-edge European companies. Academy of Management Journal, forthcoming.

Shein, E. H. (1987). Process Consultation, vol. II. Lessons for Managers and Consultants. Reading, MA: Addison-Wesley.

Watkin, K. E., and Marsik, W. J. (1993). Sculpting the Learning Organization. San Francisco: Jossey-Bass.

Yin, R. K. (1994). Case Study Research: Design and Methods. Beverley Hills, CA: Sage Publications.

Tables

Table 1

1. *Variable 130: SRPP benefited from a prevailing constructive culture focused on national issues and resistance to the imposed war*
2. *Variable 132: Most SRPP employees were convinced that helping each another to learn would lead to a national benefit*
3. *Variable 140: Team learning for problem-solving was strongly encouraged and accepted by employees*
4. *Variable 144: The project succeeded because employees were prepared to accept changes in their working conditions*
5. *Variable 145: Changes in the environment and society, especially the war and economic sanctions, helped employees to change their attitude to learning from experience*

Table 2

1. *Variable 128: The project was organized to gain the commitment of its workers to managers*
2. *Variable 129: The project was organized to enhance workers' commitment to learning through doing*
3. *Variable 138: In this project the belief of personal mastery was encouraged*
4. *Variable 141: All of the working stages were defined and the relationships between stages were planned*
5. *Variable 142: Everyone was briefed on how to do his job before starting each function*

Table 3

1. *Variable 131: The project succeeded in encouraging openness and information transparancy*
2. *Variable 134: Managers prepared staff to accept that obtaining more knowledge during the project would lead to a better life in the future*
3. *Variable 137: In this project, transfer of knowledge was quick and efficient*
4. *Variable 139: In this project, people shared their ideas with others clearly*
5. *Variable 146: Employees believe that completion of the project was necessary because foreign experts had left the country*

Table 4

1. *Variable 133: Employees were convinced that construction of the project will lead to industrial self-sufficiency*
2. *Variable 135: Employees were convinced that their salary was better than for other Tavanir projects*
3. *Variable 143: Employees were convinced that success of the project was based on predicting actions and steps that should be taken 30*
4. *Variable 147: Employees were convinced that completion of the project was necessary to satisfy national self-confidence*